NEIL ARMSTRONG

By Tim Goss

WORLD ALMANAC® LIBRARY

Please visit our web site at: www.worldalmanaclibrary.com
For a free color catalog describing World Almanac® Library's list
of high-quality books and multimedia programs, call 1-800-848-2928 (USA)
or 1-800-387-3178 (Canada). World Almanac® Library's fax: (414) 332-3567.

Library of Congress Cataloging-in-Publication Data

Goss, Tim, 1958-
    Neil Armstrong / by Tim Goss.
       p. cm. — (Trailblazers of the modern world)
    Includes bibliographical references and index.
    Summary: A biography of the first man on the moon, covering his youth, his career as an astronaut,
and his life after NASA.
    ISBN 0-8368-5075-0 (lib. bdg.)
    ISBN 0-8368-5235-4 (softcover)
    1. Armstrong, Neil, 1930-—Juvenile literature. 2. Astronauts—United States—Biography—Juvenile
literature. [1. Armstrong, Neil, 1930-. 2. Astronauts.] I. Title. II. Series.
    TL789.85.A75G76   2002
    629.45'0092—dc21
    [B]   2002024172

This edition first published in 2002 by
World Almanac® Library
330 West Olive Street, Suite 100
Milwaukee, WI 53212 USA

This edition © 2002 by World Almanac® Library.

Project editor: Mark J. Sachner
Design and page production: Scott M. Krall
Photo research: Diane Laska-Swanke
Editor: Betsy Rasmussen
Indexer: Walter Kronenberg
Production direction: Susan Ashley

Photo credits: © AP/Wide World Photos: 4; © Bettmann/CORBIS: 5 top, 9 bottom, 10 bottom, 15, 16, 23 both, 24 top, 27
all, 28, 36 top, 40 bottom left, 41; © CORBIS: 17 both; © Hulton-Deutsch Collection/CORBIS: 11; © Latif/Reuters/Getty
Images: 42 top; © Museum of Flight/CORBIS: 9 top; NASA: cover, 5 bottom, 6, 19, 24 bottom, 25, 26 both, 29, 30, 31, 32,
34, 37, 38 both, 39, 40 top and bottom right; © NASA/Getty Images: 33, 36 bottom; Ohio Historical Society: 7, 8, 12, 20;
© Underwood & Underwood/CORBIS: 10 top; © Wilson/Reuters/Getty Images: 42 bottom

Printed in the United States of America

1 2 3 4 5 6 7 8 9 06 05 04 03 02

Words that appear in the glossary are printed in **boldface**
type the first time they occur in the text.

CHAPTER 1

THE FIRST MAN ON THE MOON

On July 20, 1969, more than a half billion people around the world stared at their television screens in amazement as astronaut Neil Armstrong slowly made his way down the ladder of the *Eagle* **lunar module** and became the first person ever to walk on the Moon. Cheers from around the world erupted when Armstrong's feet finally touched the Moon's surface. With just one step, Neil Armstrong became one of the most celebrated astronauts in history. How Armstrong actually got to the Moon is a long, colorful tale of many important, small steps.

On July 20, 1969, Neil Armstrong became the first person to set foot on the Moon.

THE SPACE RACE BEGINS

When World War II ended in 1945, the United States and the **Soviet Union** were the world's two great superpowers. During the 1950s, both countries spent millions of dollars researching and developing faster and safer modes of air travel. This led to new jet planes that were used by both the military and civilians, but scientists from both countries were looking far beyond the Earth's own atmosphere. They wanted to develop rockets and capsules for travel in outer space.

On October 4, 1957, the Soviet Union shocked the world when it successfully launched the first **artificial satellite** into **orbit**. Scientists from all over the world were amazed as *Sputnik* circled Earth every ninety-six minutes. U.S. scientists were also worried that similar Soviet satellites could be used for aggressive military purposes. The United States responded quickly by organizing a new national space program. In 1958, the National Aeronautics and Space Administration (NASA) was established with one urgent purpose in mind—to develop the world's best new rockets, satellites, and space exploration vehicles.

In 1961, President John F. Kennedy promised that the United States would land astronauts on the Moon before the end of the decade.

THE RACE TO THE MOON

On May 25, 1961, President John F. Kennedy challenged the United States with a bold proposal. In a speech to Congress, Kennedy said, "I believe that this nation should commit itself to achieving the goal, before this decade is out, of landing a man on the Moon and returning him safely to the Earth." Although nobody knew it at the time, that man would be Neil Armstrong.

NEIL ARMSTRONG, SUPER PILOT

From his early childhood on, Neil Armstrong had one great passion—flying. During college, Neil studied

President Kennedy examines an early model of the *Apollo* command module.

aeronautical engineering and also served as a fighter pilot for the U.S. Navy. In his professional life, Neil worked as a test pilot, a flight researcher and designer, a professor of aeronautical engineering, and, of course, a NASA astronaut. The story of the "super pilot" Neil Armstrong is indeed a tale of a genuine American trailblazer and hero.

Before becoming an astronaut, Neil Armstrong was a renowned navy test pilot.

CHAPTER 2

Neil Alden Armstrong was the first of three children of Stephen and Viola Armstrong. He was born on August 5, 1930, at his grandparents' farmhouse near Wapakoneta, Ohio. Neil's father, Stephen, was an **auditor** for the state of Ohio during Neil's formative years. Mr. Armstrong reviewed the financial records of different counties in Ohio. On the average, it took Mr. Armstrong and his partners about one year to review a county's financial records. As a result, the Armstrongs moved sixteen times within Ohio during Neil's first fifteen years.

Neil Armstrong as a youngster in Ohio.

The Great Depression

The Stock Market Crash of 1929 marked the beginning of the United States' most difficult economic period—the Great Depression. Between 1929 and the early 1940s, millions of Americans lost their jobs when many businesses shut down. Banks across the country closed their doors when customers rushed to withdraw their savings. As an auditor for the state of Ohio, Stephen Armstrong was able to keep his job throughout the Great Depression.

The Armstrong
family home in Ohio.

NEIL'S FIRST LOOK AT FLYING

In 1932, Stephen Armstrong worked in Cleveland, Ohio. From time to time, Mr. Armstrong took two-year-old Neil to look at the planes at the Cleveland Airport. Mrs. Armstrong remembers that Neil was always "so fascinated that he was never ready to leave [the airport]." On one occasion, Neil and his father saw the National Air Races at the airport. Many new and old planes raced across the sky and performed daredevil stunts before the thrilled audience.

When Neil was six years old, his family lived in Warren, Ohio. One Sunday morning, Neil and his father went out to the local airport before church service. Mr. Armstrong had heard that a Ford Tri-Motor plane was making a brief stop at the airport. The shiny metal plane, nicknamed the *Tin Goose*, amazed Neil and his father. When a pilot offered to take Neil and his dad for a ride, the young boy's eyes bulged with excitement. Neil was fascinated by the flight. His father, on the other hand, had a different opinion. ". . . I was scared to death," recalled Mr. Armstrong. ". . . those old Ford Tri-Motors . . .

really rattled." After their ride, Neil and his father tried to sneak back home. "We were supposed to be at church," said Neil, ". . . but . . . later my mother caught us, just because of the guilty, and probably excited, looks on our faces."

SUPERSTUDENT AND FLYING FANATIC

When Neil was a very young child, his mother spent many hours showing magazines to him and reading books to him. During first grade, Neil read a total of ninety books! His teacher was so impressed that she decided to have him skip second grade. As far as his

The speedy *Super Sportster*, one of the aircraft two-year-old Neil Armstrong saw at the 1932 National Air Races in Cleveland, Ohio. At the time, this plane held the world speed record of 294 miles per hour (473.8 kilometers per hour).

The U.S. Navy's Fifth Fighting Squadron entertains the crowd at the 1937 National Air Races in Cleveland.

When Neil Armstrong was six years old, he and his father went for a ride in a Ford Tri-Motor *Tin Goose* passenger plane.

Passengers enjoying a flight aboard a *Tin Goose*.

teachers and family were concerned, Neil's reading skills were as far-reaching as the stars in the sky.

Neil loved to read books about the Wright Brothers. In the early 1900s, these inventors owned a bicycle shop in Dayton, Ohio. They designed their own man-carrying gliders and motor-powered air machines. On December 17, 1903, the Wright brothers tested a new engine-powered air machine in Kitty Hawk, North Carolina. On that day, Orville and Wilbur Wright became the first people ever to fly successfully in an airplane. Little did Neil imagine that, less than seventy years later, he would be making flight history, too—this time on a trip all the way to the Moon.

After flying on the *Tin Goose*, Neil's fascination with planes and flying grew by leaps and bounds. He read *Air Trails* and other flying magazines and spent many hours building and flying model airplanes.

Neil Armstrong: SuperStudent and Fortune-Teller

Just days before the *Apollo 11* launch, *The National Observer* interviewed Neil's high school science and math teacher, Mr. Grover Crites, about Neil Armstrong, the student:

He read everything on aviation that he could get his hands on. . . . [Neil] was a dreamer . . . [and] we expected to hear from him [later in life]. Science was his field and love. I expected him to make a contribution. He was always thinking far ahead of himself, but I never expected the Moon.

On a fall evening in 1946 during his senior year, Neil visited Mr. and Mrs. Crites at their home. Looking up at the harvest Moon, Mr. Crites asked Neil what he would like to do after graduating from high school. Neil quickly replied, "Mr. Crites, some day I'd like to meet that man up there."

Pioneers of powered flight and fellow Ohioans Wilbur Wright (left) and his brother Orville were Neil Armstrong's childhood heroes.

Young Neil Armstrong in his band uniform. Neil played the baritone horn. He also studied piano.

When the family moved from St. Mary's to Upper Sandusky, Ohio, Neil and his new friends often built model airplanes and flew them out of the second-story windows of the Armstrong home. To pay for his flying hobby, ten-year-old Neil got his first job mowing the lawn at the local Mission Cemetery. Later, Neil took a job at Neumeister's Bakery, where he "made one hundred and ten dozen doughnuts every night." Neil later said, "I probably got the job because of my small size; I could crawl inside the vats at night and clean them out."

When Neil was fourteen years old, the Armstrongs moved back to Wapakoneta, Ohio. They settled in a white, tree-shaded, two-story house in a quiet family neighborhood. In the fall of 1944, Neil entered Blume High School as a sophomore. His younger sister, June, and younger brother, Dean, attended the local elementary school.

During his three years at Blume High School, Neil held several jobs in order to earn money for his growing passion for flying. Neil first worked at the West End Market as a stock boy. Later, he worked at Bowsher's Hardware Store and then took a job at Rhine and Bradings Pharmacy. Neil was a good student who often got As in science and math. In fact, he was so good at science and math that he was asked to temporarily teach the courses when his teacher was sick. Outside of school, Neil taught himself calculus and also was a member of the local Boy Scouts troop. He played baritone horn in the high school band and orchestra and sang in the high school glee club. During his senior year, he became the vice president of the school council and began to spend

The Danger of Flying

One day during his high school years, Neil came upon emergency vehicles at a crash scene. He quickly recognized the crashed plane from his flight school. Neil learned that the pilot who had died in the crash was one of his flight school buddies. For the next two days, Neil spent many quiet hours alone in his room. On his sixteenth birthday, Neil earned his student pilot's license—well before receiving his driver's license.

more of his free time at the Port Koneta airport. Neil's father said that Neil "never had a girl. He didn't need a car. All he had to do was get out to that airport."

When Neil was fifteen, he began to take flying lessons at the airport. To pay for his lessons, Neil worked at Rhine and Brading's pharmacy on Main Street.

Before school each day, Neil went to the pharmacy to sweep the floors. After school and on Saturdays, Neil stocked the pharmacy shelves, helped customers find store items, and did other odd jobs at the pharmacy—earning no more than forty cents an hour. During his free time, Neil found rides to the airport to watch the planes take off and land. He also spent time studying the designs of different airplanes and cleaning planes in order to earn extra money. On occasion, Neil would even take a flying lesson with a private instructor pilot, but many hours of hard work passed between his lessons. Back then, it took Neil about twenty-three hours of work at the pharmacy to earn the nine dollars needed to pay for each lesson.

THE WONDERFUL MR. ZINT!

Was it always Neil Armstrong's destiny—from the day he was born—to be the first person on the Moon? We will never know the answer to that question. We do know that Neil Armstrong was very lucky to have Jacob Zint as a neighbor in Wapakoneta. Mr. Zint was an amateur astronomer who built a home observatory on top of his garage. The dome of his observatory had a diameter of 10 feet (3.05 meters) and moved on roller skates. Mr. Zint also made telescopes in his spare time. His best telescope had an eyepiece that brought the Moon one night to within 900 miles (1,448 kilometers) of young Neil's curious eyes. "Most of the kids would look for two or three minutes and that would be enough," recalls Mr. Zint. "But Neil would look and look and look. . . . When he looked through that telescope, that's all he wanted . . . he was all business."

COLLEGE AND NAVY LIFE

The year 1947 was a very important one for Neil Armstrong. After graduating from Blume High School in the spring, Neil set his sights on beginning college in the fall. At age seventeen, Neil had already learned many important lessons from his family and close friends. More than anything, Neil knew how important it was to "do a useful job and do it well." College seemed like a perfect way for Neil to eventually find that "useful job."

Both Neil and his parents knew that college tuition was very expensive. During Neil's senior year of high school, he applied to the navy's college **scholarship** program. Several months later, a letter from the U.S. Navy informed Neil that he had been accepted. After Neil read the letter, he shouted with joy to his mother. He knew that the scholarship would give him a chance to study flight engineering. He also knew that by joining the navy, he would get an opportunity to fly the newest and fastest jets in the world. When Neil read the letter, his mother was in the basement, grabbing a jar of fruit off a shelf as she prepared to bake some pies. "He scared me to death," remembered Mrs. Armstrong. "I dropped a jar of blackberries on my big toe. I must have broken the toe—it was black and blue for weeks." When Neil told his mom the good news, Mrs. Armstrong hugged her son proudly. Deep in her heart, she felt confident that Neil had truly heard his life's calling.

The invasion of South Korea by Communist North Korean forces in 1950 outraged the non-Communist world.

A CALL TO DUTY

In the late 1940s, the communist government of North Korea threatened to invade South Korea. The

United Nations responded in 1950 by sending a multinational military force—including U.S. soldiers—into South Korea. Just five years after World War II had ended, the United States was once again involved in a war.

In the fall of 1947, Neil began studying aeronautical engineering at Purdue University. In 1949, however, after just three semesters of engineering, the United States called all military personnel into active duty to fight in Korea. Neil moved to Pensacola, Florida, for flight training as a naval air **cadet**. He chose to be a solo fighter pilot, because, at the time, he did not "want to be responsible for anyone else." After a short training period, the twenty-year-old Neil became

In a broadcast speech, President Harry Truman outlines the U.S. response to the North Korean invasion. The United States would officially enter the war on June 30, 1950.

Neil's First Brushes with Death

Flying a Panther fighter jet in the Korean War was a very dangerous job. During one mission, Neil's jet was hit with bullets from an enemy fighter. Armstrong said, "Flak hit the plane, making it unsafe for landing. The plane's control system was knocked out; I could stay in the air, but couldn't land." Neil calmly guided his jet fighter to friendly territory and then parachuted to safety.

During another mission in North Korea, a cable that the enemy had strung across a valley clipped off a large part of Neil's jet's wing. Once again, he managed to guide the crippled plane out of enemy territory and return safely.

the youngest member of his flight **squadron**. Fighter Squadron 51 used the **aircraft carrier** *Essex* as a home base and an airstrip for takeoff and landing on bombing **missions** aimed at land targets, such as trains, tanks, and bridges. During the Korean War, Neil flew a total of seventy-eight combat missions and earned three flying medals for his work.

As a navy pilot in Korea, Neil Armstrong flew the Grumman F9F Panther fighter jet.

When Neil's duty with the navy ended in 1952, he returned to Purdue University to finish his aeronautical engineering studies. During the next two years, Neil taught math classes, played in music groups, joined a college fraternity, and made some extra money on the side by delivering morning newspapers. One morning while working on his paper route, Neil met Janet Shearon, a home economics student from Evanston, Illinois. Over the next two years, Neil and Janet became good friends, thanks in part to the fact that they both were interested in flying.

In January 1955, Neil graduated from Purdue with a bachelor of science degree in aeronautical engineering. Neil was anxious and ready for a professional career as a pilot and flight researcher. He had already proven to himself and others that he was a talented pilot. In fact, Neil Armstrong would turn out to be the exact kind of pilot that the U.S. space program was looking for.

THE U.S. SPACE PROGRAM

In 1955, Neil accepted a job as a researcher and test pilot at the Lewis Flight Propulsion Laboratory in Cleveland, Ohio. Although Neil was happy to be close to home again, his heart was still set on outer space. One day while talking to the director of his research laboratory, Neil said, "I think space travel will someday be a reality. When it is, I'd like to be part of it." Just a few months later, Neil's dream to fly in space moved one critical step closer to reality. He transferred to Edwards Air Force Base in California for a new job as a test pilot and flight researcher.

The massive wind tunnel (center of photograph) at the Lewis Flight Propulsion Center in Cleveland, Ohio. The tunnel was used to test engine parts for the experimental aircraft that Neil Armstrong and other test pilots flew.

A WEDDING PROPOSAL

When Neil packed up his bags and drove to California in the summer of 1955, he decided to take a detour north to Wisconsin, where his college friend Janet Shearon was working as a summer camp counselor. During the past few years, Neil and Janet had kept in touch through many letters and phone conversations. When Neil met Janet at the

The former Janet Shearon and Neil Armstrong on their wedding day in January 1956, in California.

camp, he asked her to marry him and move to California. Neil tried to convince Janet to say yes by telling her that the government would pay him six cents a mile (instead of four cents a mile) for the trip to California if they traveled together as husband and wife! This is a good example of how serious and businesslike Neil Armstrong was with every aspect of his life. Although Janet was definitely interested in marrying Neil, she said she would need more time to think about it, so she sent him off to California on his own. In January of 1956, Neil and Janet were finally married. In 1957, their first son, Eric (Ricky), was born. Two years later, in 1959, their daughter Karen was born.

Neil the Flight Control Designer

The X-15 plane was the fastest plane ever designed. When Neil flew test flights with the X-15, he noticed that it was very hard to control the plane at high speeds as it accelerated. As the speed increased, the pilot had to pull back on a driving stick. This lowered the plane's rudder, causing the plane to quickly change its position and fly more like a rocket than a plane. After several test flights in the X-15, Neil began to envision a new flight control system that involved a smoother rudder-control mechanism. After some time, Neil finally designed a new flight control system that made it much easier for the pilot to control the X-15 at higher speeds. In a sense, Neil's flight control system was similar to the automatic steering system used today in many cars. It made it much easier to smoothly adjust the rudder as the plane's speed increased.

THE X-15 PROGRAM

One of Neil's first assignments at Edwards Air Force base was to test pilot the new X-15 **hypersonic**, rocket-powered plane. The X-15 jet, which was really half plane, half rocket, was the closest vehicle ever to being a spaceship. Armstrong flew a total of seven test missions with the X-15, reaching speeds of 4,000 miles per hour (6,437 kph) and soaring to heights as great as 57 miles (92 km) into the sky. ". . . [A]s a civilian research pilot of the X-15 rocket plane . . . I had . . . the time of my life," said Neil. "I flew up to the edge of space seven times. . . . You can see the Earth below you from that height, and you think: this is the real thing—like fantastic."

Although Neil was a superb test pilot, he was also an excellent flight-control researcher and designer. He knew the X-15 plane very well. His aeronautical engineering background helped him research and develop a better **flight control system** to fly the hypersonic plane. William H. Dana, a test pilot at Edwards Air Force Base, admired Neil's research. ". . . everyone else was telling Neil this didn't look like a very practical concept," said Dana. "[B]ut eventually it went into the number three X-15 . . . [which] was the one that set all the altitude records, and one of the reasons it flew better was because of this . . . [new] flight control system. Neil was the X-15 pilot who recognized the merit of that concept and pursued it."

A Family Tragedy

In 1961, two-year-old Karen Armstrong bumped her head while playing at a park. Although the injury seemed not to be life threatening, Karen's health worsened during the next several weeks. Neil and Janet decided to take Karen to a hospital in Los Angeles, where doctors discovered a brain tumor that could not be surgically removed. For six weeks, Karen received outpatient therapy, and during the next several months, her health seemed to steadily improve. But soon she began to experience recurring problems trying to focus her eyes. Doctors tried new treatments for Karen, but her condition quickly worsened. On January 28, 1962—the date of Neil and Janet Armstrong's sixth wedding anniversary—Karen Armstrong died, just a few days before her third birthday.

NASA's First Three Projects

After NASA was established in 1958, it created three different projects that were designed to eventually fulfill President Kennedy's promise of landing a person on the Moon. These projects overlapped each other during the 1960s as NASA developed new goals and technology for sending astronauts to the Moon.

Mercury Project
Time Period: 1958 (when NASA was established) to 1963
Number of Missions: 6
Mission Purpose: Study how a human being reacts to flight in outer space.
General Description: Each mission had one astronaut.

Gemini Project
Time Period: January 3, 1962 to 1966
Number of Missions: 10
Mission Purpose: Study how longer space flights affected astronauts; provide a hands-on training environment for astronauts to fly space capsules without the aid of computers at **Mission Control**.
General Description: The *Gemini* capsule was much larger than the *Mercury* capsule.

Apollo Project
Time Period: 1961 to 1975 (last lunar landing in 1972)
Number of Missions: 12
Mission Purpose: Fulfill President Kennedy's promise of landing human beings on the Moon.
General Description: Each manned mission had three astronauts and a craft that was twice as big as the *Gemini* capsules.

Neil's work at Edwards Air Force Base was so impressive that he received the Institute of Aerospace Sciences' Octave Chanute Award in 1962. When the X-15 program finally ended, Neil became a consultant for a new jet plane project called the Dyna-Soar X-20. This new aircraft, which some pilots called the "ultimate" spacecraft, would be part airplane, part spacecraft. While Neil worked on the Dyna-Soar project, he began paying close attention to NASA's new astronaut program, the *Mercury* Project. In 1962, he decided to leave the Dyna-Soar project and apply for a position with NASA's second group of astronauts destined for the *Mercury* Project. Leaving the test pilot program was not an

NASA test pilot Neil Armstrong taking delivery of a new X-15 rocket airplane at Edwards Air Force Base in California.

easy decision for Neil, but he did know that if he ever wanted to fly in outer space, he would have to be part of Project *Mercury*, NASA's new program to study how astronauts react to flight in outer space.

Neil Armstrong in the cockpit of the X-15 rocket plane, which could reach speeds of over 4,000 miles per hour (6,437 kph) and a maximum altitude of 57 miles (92 km).

CHAPTER 5

ASTRONAUT NEIL ARMSTRONG

NASA astronauts pose with a model of the Project *Gemini* launch vehicle. Armstrong is in the second row, second from the left.

Neil Armstrong in training for his *Gemini* mission.

In 1962, NASA selected a second group of astronauts for a new program called the *Gemini* Project. This program continued to study the effects of space travel on astronauts and also trained the astronauts to fly in outer space without the help of the Mission Control computers. Each *Gemini* astronaut had to be a jet pilot with a college degree, have at least one thousand hours of flying experience, and meet other physical requirements. Neil was worried that NASA would not accept him because he was no longer active in the military. Luck was on Neil's side when he became NASA's first civilian astronaut.

The Armstrongs moved to El Lago, Texas. This quiet town, which was close to NASA's Manned Spacecraft Center in Houston, was home to many NASA astronaut families. In 1963, the Armstrongs welcomed the arrival of their second son, Mark. During Neil's first two years in Texas, he and his fellow astronauts spent a lot of time in the classroom. They learned important details about the new *Gemini* spacecraft. They also studied space navigation, including how to use both the stars and specialized computers for traveling in outer space.

COMMANDER NEIL ARMSTRONG

Neil's first job as an astronaut was to serve as the backup command pilot for the

Neil Armstrong being briefed on the new *Gemini* spacecraft.

Gemini 5 flight scheduled for August 1965. In 1966, Neil took his first primary commander assignment when he and Air Force Major David R. Scott were chosen for the *Gemini 8* mission. *Gemini 8*'s goal was to fly into Earth orbit and perform a **docking** with another ship called the *Agena* target craft. Major Scott was also scheduled to take a two-hour space walk during the mission. In order to practice for this mission, the crew had to spend many hours training on NASA simulators. These training machines were designed to look and act just like an actual spacecraft.

GEMINI 8
TAKES OFF

Neil's first flight into space aboard *Gemini 8* was scheduled for March 15, 1966. Just before the scheduled launch, NASA technicians tested the spaceship and discovered some mechanical prob-lems. NASA decided to delay the launch one day while technicians made adjustments, including fixing one of the *Gemini 8* jet thrusters. These thrusters are rocket

Neil Talks About the *Gemini* Simulators

Neil wrote articles about astronaut training for *Life Magazine*. Here is what he said about using simulators to train for space travel:

There is no Earthly way—literally—to practice an entire Moon mission. For all our calculations and planning, it will be a voyage into the unknown, and the flight itself will be the first full-dress rehearsal. The best we can do is to break the mission down . . . to master each separate step with the help of an assortment of strange and sophisticated machines called simulators.

. . . [We] can't afford to wait until we're in trouble on an actual flight before we start figuring out ways to solve it. We have to think ahead and imagine all of the conceivable emergencies we might face . . . and then come up with the right conclusions for them without ever leaving the ground.

The *Gemini 8* crew: astronaut David R. Scott (left) and command pilot Neil Armstrong.

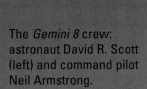

Neil Armstrong being fitted into his space suit for the launch of the *Gemini 8* spacecraft on March 16, 1966.

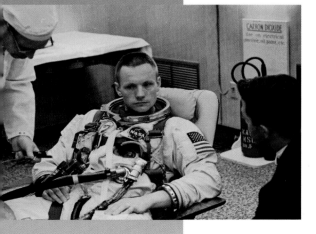

engines that are fired (or "burned") by the commander to change the ship's direction of travel. They are located on the top, bottom, and sides of the space capsule.

On March 16, 1966, at 11:41 A.M., *Gemini 8* and its crew—Neil Armstrong and David R. Scott—were launched into outer space. The *Agena* target craft was already in space and orbiting Earth. In just six minutes and nine seconds, *Gemini 8* passed through Earth's atmosphere and began its first Earth orbit. It was now time to "catch up" with the *Agena* and initiate the procedure for docking. When *Gemini 8* was in its third orbit, Neil told Mission Control, "We've got a visual on the *Agena* at 76 miles (122 km)." Armstrong and Scott continued speeding ahead to catch up with the *Agena*. Just over an hour later, they passed by the target craft and then used *Gemini 8*'s thrusters to turn the ship around—face to face with the *Agena*.

Armstrong aimed the tip of *Gemini 8* at the target docking port on the *Agena*. Then he turned on the rear thrusters and steered the *Gemini* as it slowly crept toward the *Agena*. As the two ships connected and the docking latches on the *Agena* target craft locked onto the *Gemini*, NASA's first successful space docking was completed. Everyone at Mission Control breathed a sigh of relief and cheered as Commander Armstrong announced, "Flight, we are docked. It's really a smoothie."

After the successful docking, Major Scott performed a thruster-firing maneuver to turn the two spaceships by 180°. The firing appeared to work perfectly as the two ships rotated in space. But trouble was just around the corner.

TUMBLING IN SPACE

The next communication from the *Gemini 8* came from Major Scott. He told Mission Control, "We have serious problems here. . . . We're tumbling end over end up here." Just minutes earlier, both ships had begun to spin in orbit. Commander Armstrong quickly used *Gemini*'s thrusters to stop the tumbling and undock the *Gemini* from the *Agena*. Almost immediately, the *Gemini* began rolling and wobbling even faster than before. Neil thought that one of the ship's sixteen thrusters was stuck in the "fire" position. He quickly turned off all sixteen *Gemini* thruster rockets, but the ship continued to spin. At that point, Neil fired the spacecraft's rear rockets, called retro-rockets. These were special thrusters that were supposed to be used only when the ship passed back into Earth's atmosphere during reentry. Neil's quick thinking worked like a charm, but *Gemini 8*'s problems were far from over.

A series of photos taken from the *Gemini 8* spacecraft as it maneuvers to dock with the unmanned *Agena* rocket. *Gemini 8* approaches the *Agena,*

closes in on the rocket,

and prepares for docking.

After firing the ship's retro-rocket thrusters, Neil and NASA officials knew they did not have much time. If they continued the mission, it was very possible that the reentry fuel would leak out. Soon Mission Control sent a message to Armstrong and Scott to come home immediately!

The change in flight plans made it necessary for NASA engineers to scramble to find a new ocean landing site for the *Gemini* ship and crew. Just over four and a half hours after *Gemini 8*'s successful docking in space, the capsule splashed into the sea. Although the *Gemini 8* mission did not accomplish all its goals, the successful docking in space made it a "thumbs-up" mission. In addition, *Gemini 8* showed NASA again what a calm and capable commander pilot Neil Armstrong truly was.

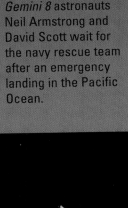

Gemini 8 astronauts Neil Armstrong and David Scott wait for the navy rescue team after an emergency landing in the Pacific Ocean.

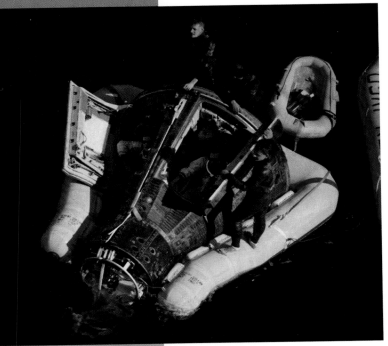

THE APOLLO PROJECT

In 1967, NASA began the *Apollo* Project. This project had one distinct goal: to land astronauts on the Moon. NASA's new program started with a tragic event during a launch simulation procedure for *Apollo 1*. Three astronauts—Virgil Grissom, Edward White, and Roger Chaffee—were killed in a fire during a practice on the **launch pad**. After the *Apollo 1* disaster, NASA waited more than a year and a half before sending another manned spacecraft into space. During that period, Neil trained for a possible flight assignment and also helped NASA engineers to design better simulators for lunar mission training.

ANOTHER BRUSH WITH DEATH

On May 6, 1968, Neil went to Ellington Air Force Base in Houston, Texas, to practice on a Moon-landing simulator. The lunar landing research vehicle (LLRV) looked and functioned very much like the actual *Apollo 11* lunar module. Neil knew the LLRV better than anyone in the entire *Apollo* project. He had already flown it twenty times and had studied its design in detail. The LLRV had no wings and moved through the air using jet- and rocket-powered engines. On May 6, Neil flew the LLRV to the normal height of about 500 feet (152 m). Then he began his lunar landing practice descent, inching the craft slowly toward the ground. At a height of about 200 feet (61 m), the LLRV suddenly began to tumble and then quickly fell toward the ground. Just before the LLRV crashed, Neil pulled an emergency handle that fired a small rocket underneath his seat. The rocket propelled Neil—still strapped into his seat—almost 300 feet (91 m) up into the sky. Neil's automatic parachute opened as the LLRV crashed into the ground. After the crash, Armstrong told reporters, "The only damage to me was that I bit my tongue."

Neil Armstrong piloting the rocket-powered Lunar Landing Research Vehicle (LLRV) at Ellington Air Force Base in Texas. Seconds later, Armstrong parachuted to safety as the LLRV spun out of control and crashed.

ASSIGNMENT: MOON

When NASA began searching for a commander for the *Apollo 11* mission, they wanted someone who could remain calm under strain. Neil Armstrong was the per-

Apollo 11 commander Neil Armstrong (right) and pilot Edwin E. Aldrin train for the *Apollo 11* mission at the NASA Manned Spacecraft Center in Houston, Texas.

fect choice. In his short flying career with the navy and the U.S. space program, Neil had already experienced four in-flight emergencies. In each case, Neil returned safely from the mission. On January 6, 1969, Armstrong had a meeting with NASA's flight crew operations manager, Donald K. "Deke" Slayton. Deke told Neil that Neil would be the commander of the upcoming *Apollo 11* mission, which would launch in either July or August. He also told him that *Apollo 11* was tentatively scheduled to be the first lunar landing mission in history. This meant that Neil and his crewmate, Edwin "Buzz" Aldrin, would be the first two humans ever to walk on the Moon. A third crew member, Michael Collins, would be the **command module** pilot. He would orbit the Moon in the command module *Columbia* while Armstrong and Aldrin used the lunar module *Eagle* for their historic journey.

The *Apollo 11* mission crew (left to right): Neil Armstrong (commander pilot), Michael Collins (command module pilot), and Edwin "Buzz" Aldrin Jr. (lunar module pilot).

First on the Moon: *Apollo 10* or *11*?

In March 1969, *Apollo 9* completed its mission of testing the lunar module in Earth orbit. Now NASA was faced with a tempting situation. *Apollo 10* was scheduled to be launched in May, 1969. By redesigning the *Apollo 10* lunar module to decrease its weight, NASA knew that this mission could actually be the first one to the Moon. Colonel Thomas P. Stafford, the *Apollo 10* commander, played an important role in convincing NASA not to change their plans for *Apollo 11* to be the first lunar landing mission. Stafford said, "There are too many unknowns up there. Our job is to eliminate as many of them as we can, and the only way we can do that is to take [the lunar module] down to 9 miles (14.5 km) or less and see how it behaves that close to the moon." Lieutenant General Samuel Phillips, director of NASA's *Apollo* program, and Dr. Thomas Paine, administrator of NASA, agreed with Colonel Stafford. As a result, the *Apollo 10* crew successfully took their command module and lunar module through the exact flight plan that *Apollo 11* would follow in July—with one exception. *Apollo 11*'s lunar module would actually land on the Moon.

APOLLO 11 FLIGHT

CHAPTER 6

Wapakoneta, Ohio

At 2:17 A.M. on July 21, Jacob Zint hopes to have his eight-inch telescope trained on the southwest corner of the Moon's Sea of Tranquility. Weather permitting, the sighting will complete an odyssey in time and space that began here 23 years ago when a small blond boy named Neil Alden Armstrong took his first peek at the Moon through Mr. Zint's lenses.

July 7, 1969, from *The National Observer* newspaper

Waking up just after 4:00 A.M. on July 16, 1969, Neil Armstrong, Buzz Aldrin, and Michael Collins knew that this day was not going to be just another day of training. In just over five hours, they would be on their way to the Moon. They ate a full breakfast and spent nearly an hour putting on their space suits. About 6:30 A.M. Houston time, the three astronauts stepped into a white van that took them to Pad 39A. Dressed in their $100,000 space suits, the *Apollo 11* crew took a slow elevator ride up the Saturn V rocket launcher toward the *Columbia* capsule.

At 4:15 A.M. that same day, Janet Armstrong awoke her two sons, Ricky and Mark. Although Mark was just six years old, he knew what was going to happen that day. "My daddy's going to the moon," he said, ". . . [and] it will take him three days." At 9:32 A.M., after the Saturn V burned more than 85,000 pounds (38,556 kilograms) of fuel in just under nine seconds, the *Apollo 11* spacecraft lifted off. Jan Armstrong and her two sons watched from a boat on the nearby Banana River. They first spotted the rocket as it climbed out from the enormous cloud of launch exhaust.

Neil Armstrong leads his *Apollo 11* crew to the "transfer" van for the 8-mile (12-km) trip to Cape Kennedy Launch Complex 39A in Florida.

How the Spacecraft Got Their Names

NASA gave responsibility for naming the *Apollo 11* command module and the lunar module to its three crew members, Neil Armstrong, Buzz Aldrin, and Michael Collins. The astronauts wanted the names to reflect the high degree of national pride and dignity that were key ingredients in this historic mission. When the *Apollo 11* patch was designed, the problem of naming the lunar module was almost immediately solved. An eagle on the patch design suggested the name "Eagle" for the lunar module. Naming the command module took a little more time. In *First on the Moon*, Neil Armstrong explained the crew's final choice:

Columbia was also a national symbol, but more importantly the choice was an attempt to reflect the sense of adventure and exploration and seriousness with which [Christopher] Columbus undertook his assignment in 1492. And, of course, there was a tie-in with the Jules Verne exploration book [From the Earth to the Moon] that turned out to be, in some ways at least, an accurate prediction of the technique and details of the Apollo 11 *flight.*

The *Apollo 11* Saturn V rocket lifts off on July 16, 1969.

"There it is! There it is!" shouted Mrs. Armstrong to her sons.

About eleven minutes later, radar from the Canary Islands confirmed that the *Apollo 11* spacecraft was in orbit, about 103 miles (166 km) above Earth. *Apollo 11*'s single J-2 engine fired, sending the ship on a direct path toward the Moon. For the next three days, the *Columbia* command module raced over 200,000 miles (321,860 km) toward the Moon. During the trip, the crew ran tests, ate regular meals, slept, exercised, and even conducted television interviews from the command module.

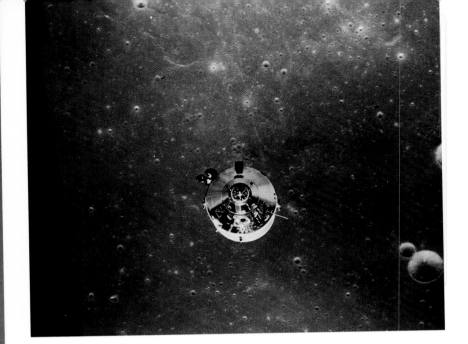

The far side of the Moon provides a compelling backdrop as the *Apollo 11* command module *Columbia* is viewed from the *Eagle* lunar module. *Columbia* has begun maneuvering for its descent to the lunar surface.

TO THE MOON

On Saturday, July 19, *Columbia* made its first **lunar pass** around the western side of the Moon. It was now time for a very important engine burn. If the *Columbia* slowed down enough, the Moon's gravity would capture the ship and send the *Columbia* into orbit around the Moon. If the *Columbia* passed too quickly, its momentum would catapult it back towards Earth. Fortunately, the *Columbia* engine burn went perfectly, and the space capsule was now in steady orbit around the Moon.

On Sunday, July 20, Neil Armstrong and Buzz Aldrin crawled through the tunnel between the command module *Columbia* and the lunar module (LM) *Eagle*. Michael Collins remained in the *Columbia* while Armstrong and Aldrin spent the next several hours preparing the LM for the undocking procedure. Each time the spacecraft passed around the far side of the Moon, radio contact with Mission Control was temporarily lost.

Just before the twelfth lunar orbit, the crew told Mission Control that they were ready for the next critical step. As the two spacecraft moved to the far side of the Moon, Collins pushed a control button that undocked the *Eagle* from the *Columbia*. The *Eagle* slowly drifted away while Armstrong and Aldrin quietly prepared for their approaching Moonwalk. After the LM came back into radio signal range with Houston, Neil Armstrong told Mission Control that "The *Eagle* has wings." Soon the LM would burn its thrusters to begin its descent toward the Moon.

"THE EAGLE HAS LANDED"

About eight minutes after both spaceships disappeared from radio signal range, the *Eagle*'s bottom engines burned for 29.8 seconds. Almost immediately, computer system overload alarms sounded aboard the *Eagle*. Back at Mission Control, panicked NASA engineers met and quickly decided to proceed with the lunar landing. When the *Eagle* came to within 1,000 feet (305 m) of the surface of the Moon, Armstrong reported that the automatic flight control system was not working correctly— the *Eagle* was moving way too fast. Neil thought the ship might crash-land into a field of boulders just below. He also noticed that the *Eagle* was quickly running out of fuel.

Always the expert commander pilot, Neil decided to turn off the automatic landing system and manually land the *Eagle*. He guided the *Eagle* over the boulders and soon found a smooth area about the size of a "big house lot" between some large craters and another boulder field. With less than thirty seconds of fuel left to burn, Neil softly guided the *Eagle* onto the Moon's surface. Everyone breathed sighs of relief when Neil reported, "Houston, Tranquility Base here. The *Eagle* has landed."

"ONE SMALL STEP"

Neil Armstrong at Tranquility Base just moments after he made his "one small step for [a] man; one giant leap for mankind."

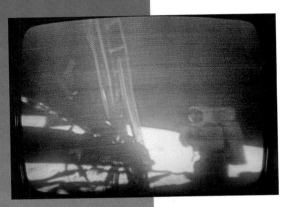

Neil Armstrong works beside the *Eagle* lunar module. Since the Moon lacks an atmosphere to create a "flag-waving" wind, a hidden support keeps the flag unfurled.

The *Eagle* crew waited anxiously as Mission Control checked for any system failures. They had to work very quickly. If they decided to abort the Moonwalk, the best times to do it would be at the three-minute and twelve-minute points after the landing. As the *Eagle* passed all systems tests, Michael Collins and the *Columbia* disappeared into orbit behind the Moon.

Back on Earth, Jan Armstrong, her sons Ricky and Mark, and close friends waited for the final "Go" from Mission Control. More than six hours after landing on the Moon, Neil Armstrong finally passed through the exit hatch on the *Eagle* and began climbing down the ladder. Neil had to move very carefully in his heavy PLSS outfit. It was critical that the space suits remained in perfect condition because the Moon's temperatures could vary between 250°Fahrenheit and –250°F (121°Centigrade and –157°C). At 9:56 P.M. Houston time, Neil jumped from the bottom platform and landed on the surface of the Moon. With a calm voice, Neil told the world, "That's one small step for a man, one giant leap for mankind."

Fifteen minutes later, Buzz Aldrin joined Neil on the Moon. During the next two hours, the astronauts ran a number of experiments and collected many Moon rock samples to take back home. Neil told Mission Control that the Moon's surface was powdery and that it was very easy to move around on. After speaking with President Nixon and planting a U.S. flag and a plaque on the

Astronaut Edwin E. Aldrin Jr. walks on the Moon. Notice the astronauts' footprints in the foreground.

Moon, the two astronauts' Moonwalk came to an end. They loaded the *Eagle*'s cargo bay with Moon samples and climbed back into the LM to begin a scheduled five-hour rest.

GOING HOME

At 12:55 A.M. Houston time, the *Eagle* began a very smooth liftoff from the Moon. More than four hours later, it successfully docked with the *Columbia* command module. For the next sixty hours, the *Apollo 11* crew sailed through space toward the Earth. As the spacecraft sped home, each astronaut took a turn sending a special message of thanks and appreciation. Neil sent the following message to people on Earth:

"The responsibility for this flight lies first with history and with the giants of science who have preceded this effort. Next, with the American people, who have, through their will, indicated their desire. Next to the four administrations and their Congresses for implementing that will; and then to the agency

Why was Neil Armstrong the First *Apollo 11* Crew Member to Walk on the Moon?

The crew of *Apollo 11* first learned of their historic lunar landing assignment in January of 1969. Michael Collins would orbit the moon in the command module while Neil Armstrong and Buzz Aldrin would become the first Earthlings ever to walk on the moon. Exactly who would be the first to set foot on the moon was still not determined. Buzz Aldrin told NASA that they should make a decision as soon as possible. Finally, Deke Slayton, the head of NASA flight operations, announced that Armstrong would be the first man on the moon. Deke had two main reasons for his choice. First, Neil had more experience than anyone else on the mission. Second, it would be more convenient for Neil to leave the LM first. His seat on the *Columbia* was closer to the hatch. In addition, the hatch swung open in a direction in which it made sense for Neil to be the first astronaut to pass through.

Close-up of an astronaut footprint. Because the lunar surface experiences little erosion, footprints should remain undisturbed for thousands of years.

and industry teams that built our spacecraft. . . . We would like to give a special thanks to all those Americans who built those spacecraft, who did the construction, design, the tests and put their hearts and all their abilities into those craft. To those people, tonight, we give a special thank you, and to all the other people that are listening and watching tonight, God bless you. Good night from *Apollo 11*." (From *First on the Moon*)

A Grammar Lesson

In 1994, the *New York Times* published an article celebrating the twenty-fifth anniversary of the *Apollo 11* mission. In that article, the author discussed Armstrong's famous words as he stepped on the moon:

Everyone expected Neil A. Armstrong to say something memorable at the moment of his first footstep on the Moon, and he obliged. But something about the one small step—one giant leap quotation seemed to be missing.

The words heard and recorded at Mission Control in Houston were "That's one small step for man, one giant leap for mankind." But Mr. Armstrong said after the flight that he had intended to say "small step for a man." The space agency left the impression that the missing article had been lost because of the radio static.

In an interview in 1971, the journalist Robert Sherrod asked Mr. Armstrong if the "a" had been lost in transmission or simply forgotten. "We'll never know," the Apollo 11 commander replied, leaving one more enigma lingering about this very private astronaut.

A plaque signed by President Richard M. Nixon and the *Apollo 11* crew. It remains on the Moon today, attached to the abandoned base of the lunar module.

SPLASHDOWN, QUARANTINE, AND A HERO'S WELCOME

At 11:49 A.M. Houston time, *Apollo 11* splashed into the Pacific Ocean near Hawaii. From miles away, the aircraft carrier USS *Hornet* sped toward the capsule. Meanwhile, navy divers jumped from the navy's Rescue One helicopter and attached an orange flotation collar around the capsule. As the capsule's hatch slowly opened, **biological isolation garments** (BIGs) were passed inside. NASA wanted to be absolutely sure that the astronauts did not bring back any strange, infectious microorganisms. The astronauts scrubbed each other with **sodium hypochlorite** and then were airlifted into the helicopter and flown to the *Hornet*.

The *Apollo 11* crew went straight from the helicopter into a special van on the *Hornet*. For the next eighteen days, they remained in special protection, called quarantine, while NASA specialists checked them and the Moon rocks for any contamination. The USS *Hornet* carried the van to Hawaii. From Hawaii, a military cargo plane flew the van straight to Houston. Doctors and other scientists then monitored the astronauts' health and studied both the crew and the Moon rocks for any space contaminants.

Almost three weeks later, the astronauts and the lunar samples were declared "contamination-free." During the next two months, the *Apollo 11* crew traveled

The Great Moon Hoax

How do we know that the United States really sent astronauts to the Moon? Some skeptics believe that the lunar landings were, in fact, a hoax. They believe that these events actually took place in a movie studio and were broadcast to the world from the studio. As evidence, they point to inconsistencies with the photo angles, shading, and so on. NASA has responded to this by stating: "Between the testimony of the dozen astronauts who walked on the moon and the moon rock samples, there is more than enough proof to demonstrate that the lunar landings actually did occur."

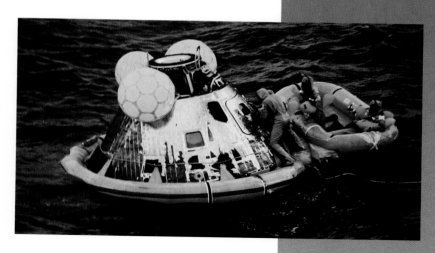

An *Apollo 11* astronaut and a Navy Rescue One crewman from the USS *Hornet* close the main hatch of the *Apollo 11* capsule. The other two astronauts wait in the life raft.

Isolated in the Mobile Quarantine Facility after returning to Earth, the *Apollo 11* astronauts rely on microphones to communicate with the crew of the rescue ship USS *Hornet* (right).

across the United States and to many parts of the world. Wherever they went, the world's new space heroes greeted audiences that roared with approval.

The lunar landing made front-page news all over the world. Even the French were impressed (below).

A joyful crowd greets the *Apollo 11* astronauts during a triumphant New York City ticker-tape parade down Broadway in Manhattan on August 13, 1969 (right).

A Private Man

"He was born on a farm in Ohio, grew up in a small town, flew to the Moon and then returned to be what he had always been, a very private person."

1994 *New York Times* article celebrating the twenty-fifth anniversary of *Apollo 11*

After *Apollo 11*'s historic mission, Neil Armstrong worked for two more years with NASA and completed his master of science studies at the University of Southern California. In his new desk job in Washington, D.C., Neil was in charge of NASA's flight division. Neil soon learned that he did not like the politically and socially charged atmosphere of Washington, D.C., but like it or not, Neil was now a national celebrity. He received many invitations to state dinners, official ceremonies, and other events. Neil found this new life unfulfilling, and, in 1971, he resigned from NASA and moved his family to a dairy farm back in Lebanon, Ohio, just 80 miles (129 km) south of Wapakoneta.

Neil Armstrong in 1971 on his first day as an aeronautical engineering professor at the University of Cincinnati.

PROFESSOR ARMSTRONG

Between 1971 and 1979, Neil worked as an aeronautical engineering professor at the University of Cincinnati, about 30 miles (48 km) from his farm in Lebanon, Ohio. Neil taught engineering classes and was involved in many research projects that were mostly related to

Neil Armstrong tosses the first pitch in the Houston Astrodome on Opening Day of the 1999 season.

Collins (left), Armstrong (center), and Aldrin standing in front of the *Columbia* command module at the Smithsonian National Air and Space Museum in Washington, D.C.

applied space technology. On one special project, Neil helped develop a miniature human heart-lung implant. The research team of scientists and physicians was headed by Dr. Henry J. Heimlich, who is best known today for his lifesaving "Heimlich maneuver" for choking victims.

BUSINESSMAN NEIL ARMSTRONG

In 1979, Neil resigned from the University of Cincinnati. During the next fifteen years, Neil took advantage of his celebrity status to pursue interesting business and personal opportunities. As a board member of several different technology corporations, Neil remained close to scientific research and development. In 1986, he was appointed as the vice chairman of the president's commission that investigated the explosion of the *Challenger* space shuttle. In 1989, Armstrong became the director of the Thiokol Corporation, the producer of the *Challenger's* solid-rocket boosters.

A RETREAT INTO PRIVACY

Neil Armstrong has always been protective of his own and his family's privacy. In 1994, the United States celebrated the twenty-fifth anniversary of the *Apollo 11* mission. Reporters from all over the country came to Lebanon, Ohio, with the hope of interviewing *Apollo 11*'s commander pilot, but Neil was nowhere to be found. Always a private man, Neil even resisted the temptation to attend a parade and celebration for him in his hometown of Wapakoneta.

Neil Armstrong so effectively protected his privacy that the news of his 1994 divorce from Janet, his wife of thirty-eight years, barely made the news. Like almost every other issue in his personal life, Neil Armstrong made sure that the divorce was strictly a private affair.

Today, Neil Armstrong leads a quiet life on his farm in Lebanon, Ohio. Neil undoubtedly wonders to this day about where human beings will fly next. Each time he looks at the Moon, he is one of only a few astronauts who can actually say, "I've been there."

Opinions About Neil Armstrong's Privacy

When the nation celebrated the historic *Apollo 11* flight's twenty-fifth anniversary in 1994, almost everyone expected Neil Armstrong to participate. Neil, however, was very determined to maintain his privacy, no matter what the reaction. The *New York Times* reported how some people responded to Neil's privacy:

After that one small step on the Moon and all the hoopla that followed, Neil A. Armstrong landed here in flat and familiar small-town Ohio. Back on Earth, the hero of the heavens . . . disappeared behind a tangle of trees off a country road where he pursued ranching, engineering, and, above all, obscurity.
   1994 *New York Times* newspaper article about the crew members of *Apollo 11*

He does not want the celebrity status that everyone thrusts on him. He wants to do what everybody else does without having to sign autographs and be interviewed. He could be the Charles Lindbergh of this era.
   Julian Scheer, former NASA spokesman

Your hometown puts on a big festival celebrating the twenty-five-year anniversary of something you did, the least you could do is show up.
   Jeff Wells, on his disappointment after the Wapakoneta twenty-five-year *Apollo 11* anniversary parade

When he chooses, he can lower the drawbridge and sally forth; but, more important, when he chooses, he can retreat with honor and dignity. Neil knows what he is doing, and he is doing it well.
   Michael Collins of *Apollo 11*, talking about the "castle" that Neil Armstrong has built around his private life

1930	Neil Alden Armstrong is born on August 5, in Wapakoneta, Ohio
1936	First airplane flight with his father Stephen in Warren, Ohio
1944	First flying lessons at Port Koneta Airport
1945	Receives his student pilot license on his sixteenth birthday
1946	Graduates from high school; joins navy cadet scholarship program; enrolls at Purdue University in aeronautical engineering
1949	Called into active duty by the U.S. Navy; flies 78 Korean War fighter missions with Fighter Squadron 51; receives 3 medals
1955	Graduates from Purdue; accepts a job at the Lewis Flight Propulsion Laboratory in Ohio and later at Edwards Air Force Base in California
1956	Marries Janet Shearon
1962	Joins NASA's astronaut program
1966	Successfully commands the *Gemini 8* mission despite problems
1968	Brush with death while training on a lunar module simulator in Texas
1969	Serves as commander of *Apollo 11*; becomes the first person to walk on the Moon on July 20
1970-1971	Serves as the head of NASA's aeronautics division; earns a master's degree
1971	Retires from NASA; moves to a dairy farm in Lebanon, Ohio
1971-1979	Works as a professor of aeronautical engineering in Cincinnati
1986	Investigates the *Challenger* shuttle disaster
1994	25th anniversary of the *Apollo 11* mission; Neil and Janet Armstrong divorce

aeronautical engineering: the science of flight

aircraft carrier: a large ship that is used as a landing and takeoff strip for planes

artificial satellite: a man-made object that is carried into space and then released into orbit around a planet

auditor: a person who studies the finances of a company, person, or government organization

biological isolation garments (BIGs): special outfits worn by *Apollo 11* astronauts to prevent the spread of contaminants from outer space

cadet: a military student

command module: an *Apollo 11* space capsule that orbited the Moon

docking: the connecting of two spaceships in space

flight control system: a grouping of devices that help to manage the navigational pattern of an air vehicle

hypersonic: a speed that is about five times faster than the speed of sound

launch pad: ground area where a spaceship takes off from

lunar module: an *Apollo 11* space capsule that carried the astronauts to and from the Moon

lunar pass: an orbit around the Moon

Mission Control: NASA flight management people who use computers and other instruments to monitor the flight of a spaceship

missions: specific tasks that someone is to complete

orbit: the curved path of a spaceship around a planet or moon

scholarship: a payment for a student's education by an organization or a special fund

sodium hypochlorite: a chemical cleansing solution used to disinfect astronaut space suits

Soviet Union: the former USSR, a country including Russia and other republics that are now independent nations

squadron: group of soldiers

TO FIND OUT MORE

BOOKS

Kramer, Barbara. *Neil Armstrong: The First Man on the Moon.* Springfield, NJ: Enslow Publishers, Inc., 1997.

Bredeson, Carmen. *Neil Armstrong: A Space Biography.* Springfield, NJ: Enslow Publishers, 1998.

Westman, Paul. *Neil Armstrong, Space Pioneer.* Minneapolis, MN: Lerner Publications Co., 1980.

INTERNET SITES

StarChild Learning Center for Young Astronomers
starchild.gsfc.nasa.gov/docs/StarChild/whos_who_level2/armstrong.html
A biography from NASA's kids' site.

Astronaut Hall of Fame
www.astronauts.org/astronauts/armstrong.htm
From the U.S. Space Camp Foundation and the Astronaut Scholarship Foundation.

Dryden Flight Research Center
www.dfrc.nasa.gov/PAO/PAIS/HTML/bd-dfrc-p001.html
NASA's biographies about the astronauts.

***Apollo 11* Mission Website**
www.ksc.nasa.gov/history/apollo/apollo-11/apollo-11.html
For everything about the *Apollo 11* mission.

The Lunar Landing Hoax
home.kurtmayer.com:8002/portal/moon.php
The site for those who doubt the authenticity of lunar landings.

The Great Moon Hoax
science.nasa.gov/headlines/y2001/ast23feb_2.htm
NASA's reply to those who doubt the authenticity of lunar landings.

About the Author

Tim Goss was born on July 4, 1958, in Milwaukee, Wisconsin. (Many years later concerned friends finally convinced Tim that the annual parades and fireworks were not in his honor.) Tim holds a B.S. in Metallurgy from the University of Wisconsin, a B.A. in English Literature from the University of Wisconsin-Milwaukee, and an M.A. in Education from the National College of Education in Evanston, Illinois. Never one to let fancy book learning interfere with his artistic side, Tim mastered the electric and upright bass and performs often in pop and gospel ensembles. Tim is a published songwriter and especially enjoys writing and teaching about music. A dedicated teacher, Tim spent ten years teaching bilingual kindergarten in the Milwaukee Public Schools, a system for which he still works as a consultant. Following his classroom experience, Tim turned his attention to writing educational texts. Tim has written for a variety of publishers about a variety of subjects, including astronomy and biography. Tim makes his home in Milwaukee when he isn't commuting to Chicago, Illinois, to spend time with his fiancée, Femi. When Tim is away, his dog Hula has the place to herself.